P9-CKQ-804

The Library of the Middle Ages™

Jerusalem Under Muslim Rule in the Eleventh Century

Christian Pilgrims Under Islamic Government

Nick Ford

The Rosen Publishing Group, Inc., New York

Published in 2004 by The Rosen Publishing Group, Inc.
29 East 21st Street, New York, NY 10010

First Edition

Library of Congress Cataloging-in-Publication Data

Ford, Nick.
Jerusalem under Muslim rule in the eleventh century: Christian pilgrims under Islamic government/Nick Ford.—1st ed.
    p. cm.—(The Library of the Middle Ages)
Summary: Explores life in eleventh-century Jerusalem for the ruling Muslims, as well as "The Peoples of the Book," Christians and Jews, who came as pilgrims or lived there.
Includes bibliographical references and index.
ISBN 0-8239-4216-3
1. Jerusalem—Juvenile literature. [1. Jerusalem—History.]
I. Title. II. Series.
DS109.916.F67 2003
956.94'4203—dc21

                                             2003002185

Manufactured in the United States of America

Table of Contents

A sixth-century mosaic map of Jerusalem

The Holy City at the Center of the World

y the year 1000, the first millennium of the Christian era, many Christians in Europe believed that the world was coming to an end and that Jesus Christ would soon come to Earth again. It seemed logical that when he returned, it would be to the place where he was last seen on Earth, Jerusalem. Many Jews and Muslims held similar beliefs, including the beliefs that the world was soon to end and that Jerusalem would be at the center of events. In the century following, many great events took place that, though they did not bring about the end of the world, certainly changed the shape of the world for the next thousand years, right up to our own time.

For Jews, Christians, and Muslims alike, Jerusalem had long been the center of the world, a place where heaven and earth, God and mankind, met. To the peoples of all three faiths, the lands around Jerusalem were the geographical center of the world they knew. To the Jews, it was important because King David had made Jerusalem the capital city of Israel 2,000 years before, and here King Solomon had built his famous temple. To the Christians, it was here that Jesus had revealed that he was the son of God, had been crucified and risen from the dead, and had sent the Holy Spirit to his disciples. To the Muslims, who revered the Jewish prophets and Jesus as well as the prophet Muhammad, it was to Jerusalem that Muhammad made his famous Night Journey to meet Abraham, Moses, and Jesus. And when the world ended, it would be in Jerusalem that God would gather together every man and woman who had ever lived, for judgment.

In Jerusalem in AD 1099, on the afternoon of June 15, a Friday, the Muslim holy day of the week when the faithful come together for prayer, the day the Christians fast, and the day the Jews prepare for the Sabbath the next day, an army of European soldiers stormed over the walls and through the gates of the Holy City. It had taken three long years of marching and fighting to get there, and a six-week siege of the city followed. Once in the city, the soldiers went into a frenzy of killing. Perhaps as many as thirty thousand men, women, and children were massacred.

Not all of those killed were Muslims. Many were native Jews and Christians. But since they all looked alike to the Europeans—brown-skinned, the men mostly wearing beards and turbans—all died together in the city where they had lived. They would have understood each others' speech, whether it was in Syrian, Greek, Arabic, or Turkish. However, these pale-skinned European foreigners spoke in a language they did not understand—French. On this Friday, June 15, 1099, the Christian Kingdom of Jerusalem was founded. The Holy City was to suffer many more wars, just as it had in the past.

The Background

The period around the year 1000 was a time of tremendous change. The great cities that were the political centers of the world stood on many centuries of culture and civilization. There was Rome, the seat of the pope, head of the Christian Church in the West; Constantinople, or Byzantium, the capital of the Byzantine (Greek) Empire, what was left of the old Roman Empire; and Baghdad, then the capital of the Turkish Empire and of the sultan, the ruler (in theory) of all Muslims.

The whole of North Africa, Egypt, Palestine, Syria, Arabia, Mesopotamia, Persia, and all but the northeast corner of Spain were under Muslim rule. Muslim armies had even reached as far as central France and Sicily. The rulers of each region were called caliphs, successors to the prophet Muhammad and therefore regarded as representatives of God on Earth. Their authority was not only religious but also political.

Although Islam began as a religion of conquest, and Muslims always tried to persuade non-Muslims to convert to Islam, it was also tolerant of other faiths. The prophet Muhammad had said, "Let there be no compulsion in matters of religion." Many of the peoples under Muslim rule at this time, especially in those countries that had been part of the old Roman Empire, were not Muslim, but Christian and Jewish. This was also true of the city of Jerusalem. Christians and Jews were known to their Muslim rulers as *dhimmi*, "protected peoples," whose sacred scripture they agreed had been inspired by God but lacked the perfection of the Koran, which God had given to Muhammad.

Muslims make a pilgrimage to Mecca to receive religious instruction in this thirteenth-century Arab manuscript.

About fifty years before the First Crusade began, a fierce tribe of Turks called the Seljuks migrated from the steppes of central Asia and carved out an empire for themselves. They seized the lands that the followers of Muhammad had converted to Islam three centuries before, but they also took territory from the Christian lands of the Byzantine Empire. They were warlike and feared wherever they went. They were not what most people, Christian, Muslim, or Jewish, would have called "civilized." Three generations before, they had been marauding nomads who only converted to Islam once they began to settle down.

The Seljuk Turks invaded what is now Iraq, and in 1055 they seized the rich and powerful city of Baghdad. A few years

Camels carry cotton across the Syrian Desert. For centuries, the trade routes between the Far East and Europe made the Holy Land a region of great economic importance.

later, they made themselves masters of what is today eastern Turkey, Syria, and Israel. During the second half of the eleventh century, Jerusalem was in the middle of continual power struggles between the Arab caliphs, ruling from Egypt; the Turkish caliphs, ruling from Baghdad; and the Greek emperors ruling from Byzantium.

Religious and political differences between the Seljuks from the north, who were Sunni (Orthodox) Muslims, and the Fatimid Arabs from the south, who belonged to the large and powerful Shiite sect, erupted into war. Jerusalem was in

A page from a fourteenth-century Arab mathematical treatise. In many areas, Islamic culture was more advanced than European culture during the Middle Ages.

the middle and, as a holy city to Muslims as much as to Christians and Jews, it was a symbol of great power and prestige to be fought over. Between 1063 and 1099, Jerusalem was involved in five wars. Leading Jewish, Christian, and Muslim scholars left Jerusalem to study and teach elsewhere in peace. Merchants and craftsmen also began to leave, as the wars were bad for trade and caravans were attacked. Pilgrims still came by the thousands, but they needed large armed escorts on the way. As law and order broke down in Palestine, bands of Bedouins robbed and killed travelers and on one occasion even entered and looted Jerusalem. Food became scarce, and prices soared. Life for everyone except soldiers and robbers became hard. In 1073, the Seljuks took Jerusalem. A little later, in 1077, Rabbi Solomon Ha-kohen ben Yehosef, wrote of them:

> They were a strange and cruel people, wearing garments of many colors . . . the chiefs among the terrible ones wearing helmets, black and red, with bow and spear and quivers full of arrows, and they trumpet like elephants and roar like the raging waters, to terrify and frighten those who oppose them.

The Dome of the Rock, built in AD 691 by Caliph 'Abd Al-Malik on the site of the Ark of the Temple of Solomon in Jerusalem

Muslim Life in Jerusalem

 n March 5, 1047, a Persian Muslim pilgrim named Abu Mu'in Nasir Ibn Khusrau arrived in Jerusalem on his way to Mecca, and he described his impressions of the city very vividly for us. He wrote that in Jerusalem there was no water except what fell as rain. The city had strong masonry walls with iron gates. Around the city there were no trees, as it was all built on rock. To Ibn Khusrau, it was a very great city, and he said that at the time of his visit there were twenty thousand men living there. If most of those men were married and had families, the whole population could easily have totaled around one hundred thousand.

Jerusalem had high, well-built, covered markets. There were many craftsmen in the city, and each craft had a market for its own wares. All the streets were paved with slabs of stone and carefully leveled so that as soon as it rained the whole place was washed clean.

Ibn Khusrau admired the great mosque of Umar at the southeast corner of the city, where the eastern city wall also forms part of its courtyard. Beyond the mosque, visitors like Ibn Khusrau had a view of a great level plain that, people said, would be the place of the Resurrection, where all humankind would be gathered together by God at the end of the world. At the edge of this plain below the city was a large graveyard, where there were many famous holy spots where people came to pray. Between the mosque and this plain was a steep valley, and Ibn Khusrau wrote that the common belief was that when you stood at the edge of this valley you could hear the cries of the damned souls in hell coming up from below. He said that he went there himself to listen but could hear nothing.

"Going south of the city for about a mile and a half, and down the valley," he wrote, "you come to a fountain of water gushing out of the rock. There are all around the spring many buildings; and the water flows on down to a village, where there are many houses and gardens. It is said that when any-one washes from head to foot in this water he will be eased of his pains, and even recover from a long illness. At this spring there are many buildings for charitable purposes . . . and the Holy City itself has an excellent hospital, provided for by great sums of money given for this purpose. Great numbers of sick people here are treated with medicine, for there are doctors who are paid to work there."

Ibn Khusrau was also impressed by the courtyard of King Solomon's Temple, in the eastern part of the city, with its magnificent gates. Through the marketplace of this quarter, he wrote, you entered the courtyard by a great and beautiful gateway over one hundred feet (thirty meters) high by seventy-five feet (twenty-three meters) across, called the Gate of King David. Set in the gateway were two doors faced with Damascene brass work, covered in gold, and ornamented with designs of many different figures. Each of the doors was forty-five feet (fourteen m) high by thirty feet (nine meters) across. This gateway had two openings into two halls. The walls of both the gateway and the halls were covered with colored enamels set in plaster, cut into beautiful patterns with an inscription set in the enamels over the gateway, giving the many honors and titles of the caliph of Egypt. When the sun's rays fell on it, Ibn Khusrau wrote, it shone with such splendor that your eyes were dazzled by the sight.

Through this gateway on the right, there were two great colonnades, each of which had twenty-nine marble pillars, with capitals and bases of colored marble. On the left and toward the north, there was another long colonnade, with sixty-four arches, supported by marble pillars. In that part of the wall there was also a gate called the Gate of Hell, which led to the place where Ibn Khusrau listened for the cries of the spirits of the damned.

Our Persian visitor went on to describe the most important Christian church. He wrote: "The Christians call it Bai'at al-Kumamah, and they hold it in great veneration." There is a story behind this. It is a Muslim joke. Literally it means the "Church of the Rubbish Heap." Its proper name in Arabic is Bai'at al-Kayamah, the "Church of the Resurrection," supposedly the place where Jesus was buried and came to life again. But the story goes that when Caliph Umar took Jerusalem from the Christian Greeks in 638, he was angered to find that the site of the Temple of Solomon had been deliberately turned into a rubbish heap by the Christians. He ordered them to clean it up and built the beautiful Dome of the Rock on the site. Since that time, the Muslims have called the Christians'

Two Arabs play chess in a tent, from a thirteenth-century Spanish manuscript.

holiest place the "Church of the Rubbish Heap" to remind them of the insult. Ibn Khusrau said of this church: "Every year, great multitudes of people from Rum [Rome, meaning the Greek Empire] come here, and the Emperor of Byzantium even comes himself, but secretly, so as not to be recognized."

In Ibn Khusrau's time, the church was considered a very large building and could hold eight thousand people. Seated in the church, he saw great numbers of priests and monks who read the gospel and said prayers by day and by night. It was built of colored marble, with ornamentation and sculptures inside. Everywhere were rich hangings of Byzantine brocade, with pictures woven on the cloth in gold thread, which filled him with wonder. There was also a painting on one of the walls in two parts, showing heaven and hell. Ibn Khusrau was sure that there was nothing else like it anywhere in the world.

Eleventh-century letters from Jewish merchants in Egypt and Palestine often deal with purchasing foodstuffs and other merchandise to sell at a profit in Jerusalem. This was mainly during the pilgrimage season. It seems that Jerusalem was regarded as a poor place for business, compared with other cities in Palestine. Rabbi Solomon Ha-kohen ben Yehosef wrote, "City life is difficult, especially in Jerusalem . . . food has to be brought from far away and there are few ways of making a living. Many rich people have come to Jerusalem, only to become poor."

An eleventh-century translucent glass jar, from northeast Persia

Some times were worse than others. In times of bad weather when crops did not grow well, or during a war or after an earthquake, life could be very hard indeed. A North African merchant, Abraham ben Isaac Al-Andalusi wrote: "The land is dead, so are its poor inhabitants, particularly those who live in Jerusalem. No one slaughters an animal here [meaning that no one could afford to eat much meat], neither for weekdays nor the Sabbath, and you can't even find a chicken."

Another Muslim, Shams Ad-Din Abu 'Abd Allah Muhammad Al Bashari, wrote a book of his travels about a century before this. He is better known by his nickname, Al Muqaddasi, meaning "the man from Jerusalem." He was a scholar and a merchant, and was very proud of his city, though he was honest enough to mention some unpleasant things about it. Even so, Jerusalem in the 900s was a far more prosperous place than Jerusalem in the 1000s, which had seen half a century of upheavals. Of all the accounts of medieval Jerusalem before the First Crusade, what Al Muqaddasi had to tell us is the most informative:

> Neither the cold nor the heat is excessive here, and snow falls only rarely . . . the buildings of the Holy City are of stone, and you will find nowhere finer or more solid construction . . . In no place will you find people better behaved. Wine is not drunk in public, and there is no drunkenness. The city has no whorehouses, public or private. The people are noted for their piety and sincerity.

Al Muqaddasi said that a castle towered over the city, one side of which was against the hillside, while the other side was defended by a ditch. He listed eight gates in the walls, all of iron: the Gate of Zion, the Gate of the Desert of the Wanderings, the Palace Gate, the Gate of the Cave of the Prophet Jeremiah, the Gate of Siloam, the Jericho Gate, the Gate of the Columns, and the Gate of the Place of Prayer of King David.

There was never any shortage of water in Jerusalem. It was a common saying then that there was no place in Jerusalem where you could not get water, nor hear the call to prayer. Few houses did not have one or more water tanks for private use, and the city also had three large main reservoirs, each one close to the public bath-houses, and these were also fed by the water drainage channels from the streets.

A cylindrical pilgrim's flask from thirteenth-century Syria. Members of all the religions of the Middle East made pilgrimages to Jerusalem.

Buying and Selling Food

Al Muqaddasi says that provisions of all kinds were of the best in Jerusalem. The markets were clean, the mosque was one of the largest in the world, and nowhere were holy places more numerous. "The grapes," he wrote, "are enormous, and there are no quinces to equal those of the Holy City."

Al Muqaddasi says that oranges, almonds and other nuts, dates, figs, and bananas were plentiful, along with milk, honey, and cane sugar. From the surrounding country-side came a sweet syrup called dibs (dates or raisins steeped in water and boiled to a paste), honey, cane sugar, plums, grapes, grapefruit, lotus-fruit, olives, and olive oil. There were artichokes, asparagus, cabbages, lupin seeds, nuts, lettuces, truffles, white bread, rice, and indigo. One could also find carpets, paper, strong double-woven woolen cloth, rope, glass jewelry and glassware, copper and brass pots, herbs and medicines, and sweets called kubbait (made from carob, sugar, almonds, and pistachio nuts) and malban (made from figs ground to a paste and dried). In particular, Al Muqaddasi praised the honey of Jerusalem, with its distinctive flavor from the flowers of wild thyme, which grew in abundance on the nearby hillsides.

From elsewhere in Palestine to Jerusalem's markets came olives, dried figs, raisins, carob, cloths of interwoven silk and cotton, soap, and kerchiefs. Muri, a fish sauce, came from Jericho. Jerusalem itself produced cheeses, raisins, apples, bananas, pine nuts, cotton cloth, mirrors, lamps, and needles. Most people who visited Jerusalem came for religious reasons. Many devout Muslims, for example, brought their children to Jerusalem to be circumcised. Many also came to die and be buried there, ready for the Day of Judgement, while those who could not afford the pilgrimage to Mecca came instead to Jerusalem. People came by the thousands, and there was always buying and selling.

A collection of bone and ivory game pieces for chess and other games, from Persia from the ninth to twelfth centuries

Food and Cooking

People cooked on ovens called furni, using charcoal or wood-burning clay. These brick stoves also served to heat the home. For baking, it was more common to take uncooked

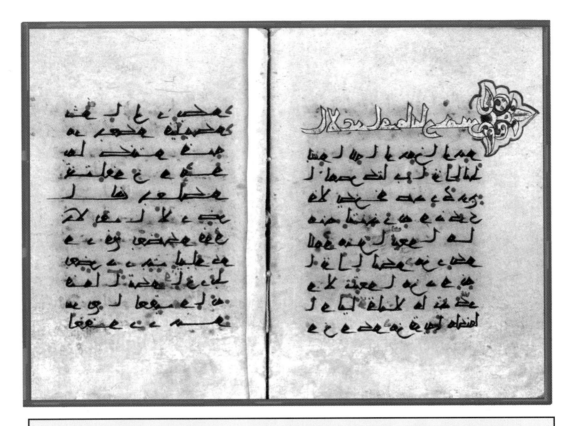

Pages from a tenth- or eleventh-century edition of the Koran, the sacred teachings of Allah as revealed to his prophet Muhammad

food to a baker's shop. The baker used another type of oven, known as the tainur. This was a hole in the ground lined with brick, into which rocks were placed. Next, dry thorns and straw or animal dung would be placed inside and set alight. When the fire burned out, the ashes were removed and loaves of bread, pies, and cakes were put in on top of the heated rocks. Then the opening would be sealed and everything left to bake.

Bread was often made with bean or lentil flour. A favorite food was baisar, beans cooked in honey and milk, usually served with meat. Bean sprouts, fried in olive oil, were often added to a dish of olives. Salted lupin seeds were a popular snack, and a specialty of the area was zullabiyyah, pastry cakes made with butter and sugar, sometimes with a sweet fruit filling.

Clothing

The use of clothing to display the social position of the wearer was very important in eleventh-century Jerusalem, as it was in the medieval world generally. Fine clothes were heirlooms, handed down from one generation to the next, to be worn only on special occasions. They not only displayed the wealth of the wearer but often *were* the wealth of the wearer. When a girl got married, half her dowry might consist of rich fabrics and expensive clothes.

Because the climate in Jerusalem was fairly mild, the inhabitants wore much the same clothes all year round, putting on thicker shoes in winter along with a heavier cloak, or a waterproof cloak during the rainy season in December. The design of clothes was very simple, and all classes of people wore much the same thing. Rich people simply had more clothes, often in bright colors, which were expensive. They were made of finer fabrics, which cost more to make, with rich embroidery. The clothes of poorer people would, by contrast, be duller in color, plain, and woven with coarser fabrics.

Many people wore a long cloak, called a ridar, all year round. For winter, they often wore a heavy, waterproof woolen cloak known as a mintar. Under this, especially when the weather was cool, people wore a durra'ah, which was a long, often multicolored, vest of linen, cotton, or wool. This was worn either open at the front or fastened with a long row of buttons. Underneath this, and usually worn at all times, was a long-sleeved cotton shirt that reached to the ankles. This shirt, known as the kisa, was usually plain white for everyday wear and colored for holidays. Women wore a closer-fitting version of the kisa and a long headscarf covering the hair and wrapping around the neck and shoulders. It could be raised to cover the face for modesty if going out in public, which people believed the Koran instructed Muslim women to do.

For headgear, men wore a turban, a long cloth wound around the head with both ends tucked inside the folds. Muslim men of importance, whether scholars or government officials, were distinguished by a tailasan, a veil of fine fabric that fell over the shoulders from the turban. In theory, only Muslim men were allowed to wear the turban and, as we shall see later, there were rules of dress intended to make Jews and Christians look recognizably different from Muslims. Except in times when the ruler was very strict, these rules were not often enforced.

Weights, Measures, and Money

The chief units of currency were the dinar and the dirhem. These coins got their names from those of the old Roman and Greek coins, the denarius and the drachma, which had been in use under the Byzantine Empire. These Greek coins remained in use until the end of the seventh century, when Caliph 'Abd Al-Malik, who disapproved of their Christian imagery, decided that there should be a new coinage that was wholly Islamic. He established a mint in Jerusalem, which produced the new coins. The new coins bore inscriptions in Arabic such as "In the name of God," "There is no God but God," and "Muhammad is the Messenger of God."

The coins were made of gold, silver, and bronze, and bore the name "Jerusalem" in both Greek and Arabic. They were often inscribed with the date, according to the Islamic calendar, that they were minted.

The dinar was a gold coin weighing slightly more than one-sixth of an ounce, and a dirhem was a smaller silver coin just over one-tenth of an ounce. Fifteen dirhems made one dinar. The main unit of weight was the ratl, which was about six pounds. Al Muqaddasi said that in the markets of Jerusalem, a ratl of cheese cost one-sixth of a dirhem. One dirhem could buy a ratl of sugar, one and a half ratls of olive oil, or four ratls of raisins. An average person earned about ten dinars per year, or about one hundred and fifty dirhems. Just as now, people found it easier and safer to write "checks" than to carry large sums of money around with them, but bank charges could be very high for this service. In 1029, a merchant complained that he had been charged more than 10 percent by a banker for cashing a check. He had to pay one dinar for every nine and a half dinars.

The Calendar, Festivals, and Feasts

Because the majority of people in Jerusalem were Christians, the calendar in general use was the Christian calendar. In the Middle Ages, most people depended on farming for their livelihood, and the seasons of the year were marked by Christian festivals. Easter heralded the spring. The Feast of Saint George (April 23) was sowing time. Whitsuntide marked the beginning of summer and the hot weather. The Feast of the Holy Cross (September 13 to 15) signaled the start of the grape harvest, and the Feast of Saint Barbara (December 4) began the rainy season. Christmas was when the cold winter weather really started, and everybody celebrated New Year's Day on the first of January by exchanging gifts.

Two important Muslim festivals, according to Al Muqaddasi, were also major events in Jerusalem. There was the Night of the Revelation of the Koran, celebrated at the main al-Aqsa Mosque adjoining the Court of King Solomon's Temple on the twenty-seventh day of the Muslim month of Ramadan. Many believed that on this night the fate of all living beings was fixed for the following year. On the fifteenth day of the Muslim month of Shabban, there was the Night of Immunity, marking the date when the direction of prayer for Muslims was changed by Muhammad from toward Jerusalem to toward Mecca. On that night, according to popular belief, the Angel of Death and the Angel of the Records received new books from God to write in and gave up their full books from the year past. In the brief interval when the old books were exchanged for new ones, there were a few moments when nothing was written down, so some people hoped that their sins might not be recorded.

Much as he loved Jerusalem, Al Muqaddasi admitted that it was far from perfect:

> Still, Jerusalem has some disadvantages. Thus it is written in the Torah that "Jerusalem is like a golden bowl filled with scorpions" . . . You will not find public bathhouses more filthy than those of the Holy City; nor in any town are provisions dearer to buy. Learned men are few and the Christians are numerous, and they are

unmannerly in the public places. In the inns, taxes are heavy on everything that is sold, for there are guards at every gate, and no one can manage to sell anything at more than a small profit.

In this city, the oppressed have no one to help them. The humble are molested, the rich are envied . . . the schools are unattended, for there are no lessons. Everywhere the Christians and the Jews have the upper hand . . .

A Muslim traveler from Spain, Abu Baqr Ibn Al-Arabi, wrote in 1090 how a criminal had avoided arrest by barricading himself in the citadel. The governor's archers were shooting at him, and then a disagreement broke out among them about the best way to capture him. They started fighting among themselves. Abu Baqr said that in any other city he knew this would have started a riot, but in Jerusalem, to his amazement, the people simply carried on with their work, their marketing, their study, their discussions of religion, quietly ignoring the whole thing. In spite of the lawlessness, there were many who felt privileged to live in the Holy City. A teacher called Amram wrote to his son in Egypt in 1055 and told him it was better to come home and eat onions in Jerusalem than chicken in Egypt.

הַלְלוּ עֶבֶד יְהוָֹה הַלְלוּ אֶת
שֵׁם יְיָ יְהִי שֵׁם יְיָ מְבֹרָךְ
מֵעַתָּה וְעַד עוֹלָם מִמִּזְרַח
שֶׁמֶשׁ עַד מְבוֹאוֹ מְהוֹלָל

This fourteenth-century Hebrew manuscript shows a rabbi holding the Torah and preaching from the pulpit of a synagogue.

Life for Non-Muslims

 hristians and Jews were regarded as the "people of the Book," those whose faith was in the same tradition of Abraham and his covenant with God, recorded in the first part of the Old Testament, but who rejected the Koran. In Muslim law, they were called dhimmi, which means "protected people." Unlike pagans, who when conquered by a Muslim army were offered the choice of conversion to Islam or death, the dhimmi were allowed to practice their own religion as before, provided that they did not try to make converts or prevent any of their faith from becoming Muslim if they wished. They could keep their existing places of worship and repair them if necessary, but they were not allowed to build new churches or synagogues.

Christians and Jews were not allowed to carry weapons, a right restricted to Muslims. Their protection was provided by the caliph, to whom they paid a special tax called *jizya* to maintain the soldiers who protected them. Of course the tax was very unpopular with the non-Muslim majority, but it was not as heavy as the taxes everyone had to pay under the old Byzantine emperors.

Every adult male Christian and Jew had to pay the jizya, except the very old and the very poor. Christian monks, who were numerous in Jerusalem, were not exempt. A special seal worn on a string around a person's neck indicated that the tax had been paid by the wearer for the current year. If a dhimm could not show it on demand, he could be in serious trouble with the authorities. The jizya was levied according to wealth. The rich dhimmi had to pay between three and four dinars, the middle classes two dinars, and the less wealthy only one dinar. The tax would increase during times of war.

Dhimmi also had to behave differently from Muslims. A Muslim could go into a church at any time, but a non-Muslim was not allowed to enter a mosque. Christians could not raise certain types of livestock, such as pigs, or publicly sell food that was offensive to Muslims. No Jew or Christian could sell alcohol to a Muslim. Their clothes had to be different, too. They had to wear yellow headgear, cloaks, and sashes, and they were not allowed to ride horses.

Jews and Christians had to step out of the way to let a Muslim pass in the street. If they were sitting down and a Muslim wanted to sit there, they had to stand and give up their seats. They could not enter a Muslim's home, but if a Muslim wanted to stay with them, they had to offer the Muslim hospitality for up to three days. And if a dhimm struck a Muslim, he could lose his rights to protection and become no better than a slave, which meant he could be killed without penalty. No Jew or Christian was allowed to keep a slave who was a Muslim.

A Muslim could not be punished with death for killing a non-Muslim, as he could be if the victim was also a

Muslim. Instead, the slayer had to pay the victim's family only half the compensation that would have been due to the family of a Muslim. Muslim law placed no restrictions on how a Jew or Christian could make a living, except that Jews and Christians could not bear arms or sell alcohol to Muslims.

A Jew or a Christian could make a will according to Jewish or Christian law, but if there were no male heirs, the property of the deceased person was shared out to the

This page from a fourteenth-century Hebrew Haggadah, a prayer book used for celebrating Passover, depicts Jews building a city for the pharaoh, a reminder of their slavery in Egypt.

family in strict accordance with the rules laid down in the Koran. Muslim law gave women more rights than Jewish or Christian law, especially with regard to inheriting property and divorce. Christian and Jewish women often appealed to Muslim courts to overturn an unfavorable judgment in their

A harvest scene from the Book of Ruth, from a fourteenth-century Hebrew manuscript published in Germany

רי: ו

שפוט ט' כיי

אמר מלוך ילך בשול' היו ויישוט ד'
מבקיעוך היון ילשב שרויה' הו ב'
התרש נבנועי' וכטב מנה' יוסר וענדד'
מכית להם יפרת' וכיון שרי מיוב
הורינו לפי שיעון מדוקון ולו נ'
בטוח מהך יוסר לוו ירעוב נפש ידזך
עתלעל הדבר שויתו' וות שוחסתה
כעל כמה שיכנה יוסר מידתה וילות
מיה שונ' ויכוו שרי מיוב לפי שול
ושב משדי מיווב' וילות ילילך מ'
ויוהרך רך וישוויו להם נשים מיוכיות
שים היה וכנהם מזיים לון היה ור'
מיכה להם לישוו נשים מיוכוות ח'
ייש נעוי' מוסב על ושם ישוט ע'
נעני' הריש כעל היושה' והישוה
רושת הדיוש' וסם הטעטרות ל'
הזכר שוותיהם ליסב שידיך לה'
לישה' וידות וגם שנהה' יון עלל
לוו' גם ילוו מדיקום שישנהה שוד'
כווהודה כן רות זה מיחון קל לזין
ותשב ושדי מיוב' עוך טעו לווה

בְּמֵי שְׁפֹט הַשֹּׁפְטִים וַיְהִי רָעָב בָּאָרֶץ
וַיֵּלֶךְ אִישׁ מִבֵּית לֶחֶם יְהוּדָה לָגוּר בִּשְׂדֵי
מוֹאָב הוּא וְאִשְׁתּוֹ וּשְׁנֵי בָנָיו
וְשֵׁם הָאִישׁ אֱלִימֶלֶךְ וְשֵׁם אִשְׁתּוֹ נָעֳמִי
וְשֵׁם שְׁנֵי בָנָיו מַחְלוֹן וְכִלְיוֹן אֶפְרָתִים
מִבֵּית לֶחֶם יְהוּדָה וַיָּבֹאוּ שְׂדֵי מוֹאָב
וַיִּהְיוּ שָׁם וַיָּמָת אֱלִימֶלֶךְ אִישׁ נָעֳמִי
וַתִּשָּׁאֵר הִיא וּשְׁנֵי בָנֶיהָ וַיִּשְׂאוּ לָהֶם
נָשִׁים מֹאֲבִיּוֹת שֵׁם הָאַחַת עָרְפָּה וְשֵׁם
הַשֵּׁנִית רוּת וַיֵּשְׁבוּ שָׁם כְּעֶשֶׂר שָׁנִים
וַיָּמֻתוּ גַם שְׁנֵיהֶם מַחְלוֹן וְכִלְיוֹן וַתִּשָּׁאֵר
הָאִשָּׁה מִשְּׁנֵי יְלָדֶיהָ וּמֵאִישָׁהּ וַתָּקָם
הִיא וְכַלֹּתֶיהָ וַתָּשָׁב מִשְּׂדֵי מוֹאָב כִּי
שָׁמְעָה בִּשְׂדֵה מוֹאָב כִּי פָקַד יְהוָה אֶת

own communities. Jews and Christians had to live in separate parts of the town, and they had their own markets. Even in the late eleventh century, both could still aspire to high office. In 1060, the governor of Jerusalem was a Jew, and his successor was a Christian.

In 1009, the new caliph, Al-Hakim, a very devout Muslim and a severe ruler whose severity, many believed, was caused by madness, gave orders that all non-Muslims were to wear black instead of yellow. He intended this as an insult to his religious and political opponents in Baghdad, who, unlike the Fatimid caliphs who ruled Palestine from Egypt, were Sunni Muslims and fond of wearing black. His decrees against non-Muslims became worse and worse. Jews were forced to wear a wooden bull's head around their necks and later a wooden block weighing twenty-four pounds. Christians had to wear a wooden cross of the same weight. Neither could use the public baths when Muslims were bathing there. All women were forbidden to visit the public baths.

Non-Muslim women had to wear special boots, one red and one black, and they had to cover their faces with a veil whenever they went out in public. No alcohol was to be sold or even made for private use. This was hard for both Christians and Jews, who needed wine for their more important religious ceremonies. Al-Hakim ordered shoemakers to stop making shoes for women. He ordered all dogs to be killed. He had many churches demolished, including the famous Church of the Holy Sepulchre, the holiest Christian place of worship in Jerusalem. Music and games were forbidden. Anyone who disobeyed Caliph Al-Hakim's strict new laws was to be punished by a flogging. Many people, Muslims included, thought Al-Hakim was mad. As the caliph ruled from Egypt, just how strictly all of Al-Hakim's laws were enforced in Jerusalem is not known. However, for any non-Muslim living in Jerusalem at that time, life must have been very difficult.

In 1021, Al-Hakim mysteriously disappeared. It is thought that he was murdered by a Muslim who believed he was a disgrace to Islam. The severity of his rule was lifted, and the traditional, comparatively liberal ways returned once more. Even so, to be a Jew or a Christian was to be a second-class citizen, whose status was below a Muslim but above that of a slave, living always with the anxiety that another Al-Hakim, or worse, might come to power and make life very hard to bear.

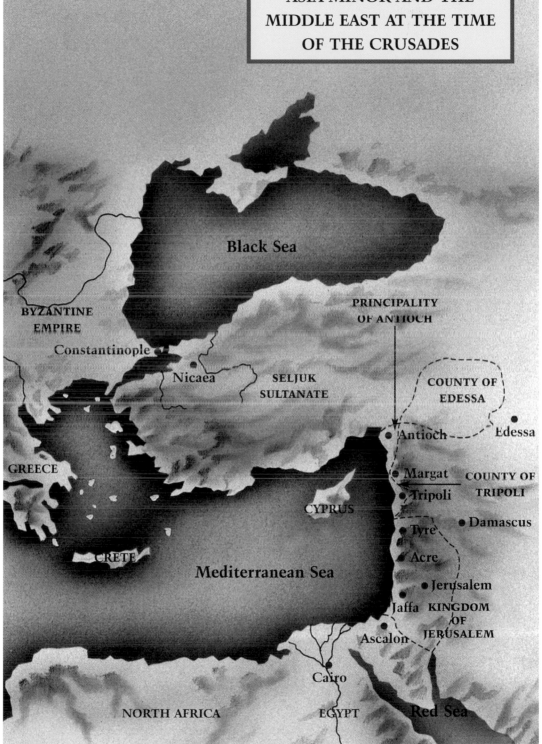

ASIA MINOR AND THE
MIDDLE EAST AT THE TIME
OF THE CRUSADES

Black Sea

BYZANTINE
EMPIRE

Constantinople

Nicaea

SELJUK
SULTANATE

PRINCIPALITY
OF ANTIOCH

COUNTY OF
EDESSA

Antioch

Edessa

GREECE

Margat

COUNTY OF
TRIPOLI

Tripoli

CYPRUS

Damascus

Tyre

CRETE

Acre

Mediterranean Sea

Jerusalem

Jaffa KINGDOM
OF
Ascalon JERUSALEM

Cairo

NORTH AFRICA

EGYPT

Red Sea

The Hebrew people on Mount Sinai, from a seventh-century French manuscript that retells the Pentateuch, the first five books of the Bible

Jewish Life

The Romans had turned Jerusalem into a Romanized city renamed Aelia Capitolina in the year AD 135 after a Jewish uprising, and Jews had been forbidden to live in the Holy City on pain of death. For nearly six centuries, until the Byzantines lost Jerusalem in the seventh century, Jews were only permitted to visit the city to lament the destruction of King Solomon's Temple and its ruined western wall, or the Wailing Wall, and only then on payment of a fixed sum of money.

There is a tradition that a number of Jews entered the city with the army of Caliph Umar, to show him where the temple had once stood. He appointed several of them to clean the rubbish from the site and afterward to protect the Dome of the Rock that he built over the spot. One team cleaned the Dome of the Rock daily with saffron, musk, and rose water, and another kept the rest of the temple site clean. These jobs were passed on from father to son, and those chosen for this service were exempt from paying the jizya. After centuries of oppression, Jews everywhere must at first have regarded the new Muslim rulers of Jerusalem as liberators. But the new liberal attitude was limited. Only seventy Jewish families were allowed to return to settle permanently. Many more, though, came to Jerusalem to visit the holy places.

Like the Christians, Jews had to pay the jizya. They were restricted as to where they were allowed to live in the city, though not as to what occupations they were allowed to follow. Al Muqaddasi said that most of the moneychangers, bankers, cloth dyers, and tanners in Jerusalem were Jews. Others were spinners of thread, weavers of cloth, shopkeepers, and scribes who made a living by copying books and documents and writing letters for those who could not write. One Jew in the eleventh century owned a flax mill in Jerusalem for making linen thread, which was sent north up the coast to Tyre to be woven into cloth, then returned to Jerusalem to be sold.

Jews were allowed to live by the rules of the Torah and to elect their own community leaders, but they were not permitted to build any new place of worship. A large cellar beneath the temple courtyard served as a synagogue, and on some holy days Jews would assemble on the Mount of Olives just outside the city. Here it was believed that the presence of God had rested for a while before leaving the city forever after the destruction of the temple. Caliph Umar also allowed them to bury their dead there. Like the Christians, Jews were not allowed to hold religious processions that interfered with the life of the Muslim community, and their funeral processions had to use the shortest route out of the city to the cemetery on the Mount of Olives, through the Zion or Siloam Gate.

The Jewish community was always small and comparatively poor. It depended on charitable donations from other Jewish communities. At the end of the tenth century,

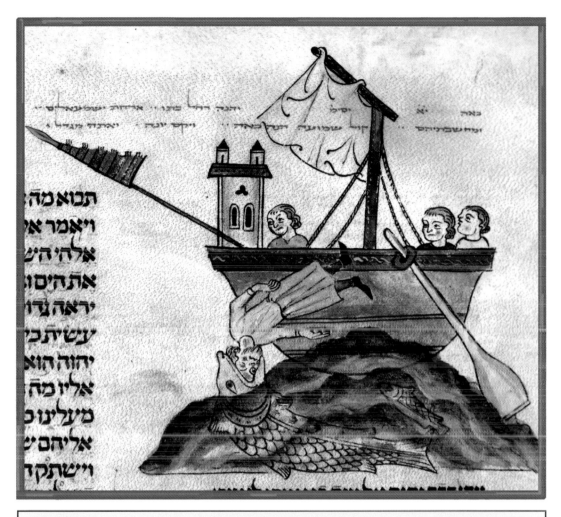

The Old Testament story of Jonah being swallowed by the whale is illustrated for this thirteenth-century Spanish Bible written in Hebrew.

Rabbi Jonah the Elder wrote a letter to the other Jewish communities asking for aid:

> Greetings to you from the faithful Lord, the Eternal City, and from the Head of Zion's academies . . . We, the Rabbainite community, a pitiful assembly living in the neighborhood of the Temple site, regret to inform you that we are constantly harassed by those foreigners

This fourteenth-century Hebrew manuscript shows the ritual of distributing unleavened bread and sweets for Passover, along with women cleaning and the ritual slaughtering of sheep.

who overrun the Temple grounds . . . life here is extremely hard, food is scarce, and opportunities for work are very limited. Yet our wicked neighbors exact exorbitant taxes and other "fees" [bribes to officials]. If we did not pay them we would be denied the right to worship on the Mount of Olives . . . these unbearable taxes and necessary, frequent bribes force us to borrow money at high rates of interest in order to avoid imprisonment or expulsion. Help us . . .

Solomon ha-Kohen ben Yehosef wrote in 1025 that the Jews of Jerusalem had to pay one hundred dinars each year as their jizya. In 1030, Solomon ben Judah recorded a money order of twenty-nine dinars sent by a wealthy Egyptian Jew who had been on a pilgrimage to Jerusalem to help support the Jewish community there. Twenty dinars out of the twenty-nine had to go to pay the jizya.

In 1059, the tax paid by a Jewish resident of Jerusalem was one hundred fifty dinars. Out of this, seventy dinars was the kharaj or land tax, forty was for the jizya, and forty was for running the city —street cleaning and garbage removal, main-

A Jewish family celebrates Passover by reading from sacred texts, from a fifteenth-century Hebrew manuscript.

taining the drainage and water supply system, repairing public buildings and fortifications, and paying officials' wages. This tax on the Jewish community in Jerusalem, however, did buy for all Jewish pilgrims the right to enter the city free of charge.

Taxes in Jerusalem seem to have been lower than in other cities under Muslim rule. This may have been partly

A Jewish wedding certificate or marriage contract from the fifteenth century

because Jerusalem was a holy city and partly because the people in it were poorer. The government may also have been trying to attract more people and more business, as the city had become depopulated after many years of war. There is evidence that some Jews may have moved to Jerusalem to escape higher taxes elsewhere. There was also a special tax on Jewish-owned shops.

The jizya was not always fairly levied. Sometimes the rate for Jews was two and a half times as much as for Christians, as in the ninth century. This may have been at a time when the governor was a Christian, or the patriarch (and perhaps even the emperor) had managed to influence the caliph to favor the Christians, who always formed a large majority in Jerusalem. Jews, like the Christians, had to wear yellow cloaks, girdles, and headgear to distinguish them from Muslims, while their slaves had to wear yellow patches on their clothing as well, one in front and one in back.

Jewish religious leaders were treated with respect by the Muslim authorities. By the eleventh century, the Jewish Academy had returned to Jerusalem. The head of the academy was in theory appointed by the caliph, but in practice the office usually passed from father to son. He officially represented all the Jews in the Holy Land to the Muslim government. Unlike any other non-Muslim, he was allowed to wear a proper full-length turban and could ride a horse (every other Jew and Christian had to use a mule or donkey). Everyone, even Muslims, had to stand in his presence. He was responsible for the official interpretation of Jewish law and for the appointment of Jewish magistrates and religious functionaries. The

This manuscript illustration shows the teaching of Hebrew scripture for Passover.

academy also had a court of appeal, made up of seven rabbis, to decide cases of Jewish law. The academy was funded both from donations by Jews and official taxes. As a religious foundation, it was a charity under Muslim law.

As well as Rabbainite (orthodox) Jews, there was a large presence in Jerusalem of a sect called the Karaites. Founded about the year 880, their leader Daniel Al-Qumusi taught that the more Jews who came to live in Jerusalem, the sooner the Messiah would come to restore the temple and put an end to the troubles of the people of Israel. They lived in their own quarter, separate from the Rabbainite Jews, outside the city walls to the southeast, near the suburb of Siloam. They believed that all Jews should study sacred scripture and that all other occupations were a waste of time. They ate no meat and drank no wine. Under Muslim law, they had the same rights as other Jews to live and worship according to their beliefs and to choose their own community leaders, but there was much ill-feeling between them and the Rabbainite Jews. This occasionally turned into violence.

Eleventh-century Byzantine mosaic on the wall of a Greek church. The style of church art in the Eastern Christian empire involved mosaics, the inlaying of colored tiles, rather than direct painting on church walls.

Christian Life

 espite the Muslim invasion and the return of the Jews, the population of Jerusalem under Muslim rule remained mostly Christian right up to the capture of the city by the first crusaders in 1099. Of the Christian population, most were Greek Orthodox, the official religion of the old Byzantine Empire.

When Arab settlers came to Jerusalem soon after Caliph Umar's conquest of Palestine, the new Muslim government found that it needed the old Byzantine Christian administration to continue to run the city. Laws had to be written down and proclamations made. Taxes had to be collected and records kept. Most of the Arabs who arrived as the new ruling class in the seventh century could not read or write. They were warriors who looked down on occupations such as farming, trading, and administration, and they did not speak the languages of the people they had conquered. For these reasons, the literate Christian monks, priests, and government officials, like the farmers and merchants, found that their old way of life was not very much changed—at first.

However, over the next four hundred years of Muslim rule, Arab scholars came to live in Jerusalem, schools of law were opened, and Arabic slowly became the main language of the city, both in government offices and in the markets. Caliphs less liberal than Umar believed that Islam forbade a Muslim to place a Christian or a Jew in a position of trust, or even to have one as a friend. So by degrees the government was taken over by Muslims. Some Jews and Christians converted to Islam to keep their jobs as officials. Others who were farmers or merchants did the same to avoid having to pay the jizya. Even then, becoming Muslim did not make them equal to those who had been Muslims from birth. The families of recent converts were often looked upon as socially inferior.

The Christian upper classes spoke Greek as their first language. The poorer classes spoke Syrian. Many of the wealthier Christians left Jerusalem during the Muslim occupation, especially during the troubles under the rule of Al-Hakim, the "Mad Caliph." Christians who came to settle in Jerusalem from elsewhere were mostly priests and monks or nuns, while those who left Jerusalem were more often people with families. Over the years, the Christian population became smaller.

There was often much cooperation between the Christians and their Muslim rulers. The Dome of the Rock, not really a mosque but a place of prayer primarily for Muslims, was built on the orders of Caliph Al-Malik by Christian Greek architects and craftsmen. Although Christians who were not Greek Orthodox did not recognize the authority of the patriarch as head of all the Christians in Jerusalem, the Muslim rulers did. The patriarch was officially

An eleventh-century mosaic shows Christ enthroned between the Byzantine emperor and his empress. The Byzantine Empire was Greek Orthodox Christian. Many of the Christians in the Holy Land came from Byzantium.

confirmed in his office by the caliph. One of these, Nicephoros, was also employed at the time as an architect of Caliph Hakim's new fortifications. The patriarchs had to pay the caliphs more than two thousand dinars each year on behalf of all the churches in Jerusalem as a special tax.

Many Christian churches in Jerusalem were built on sites connected with events in the Bible, which Muslims also revered. Different denominations prayed in Greek, Syrian, Georgian, Armenian, Arabic, Coptic, and Latin. The sound of church bells was louder than the Muslim call to prayer from the mosques, so in the eighth century one caliph ordered that the church bells be removed and wooden clappers used instead. There is one church in Jerusalem that still uses one of these wooden clappers today. Churches and monasteries in Jerusalem were supported by wealthy pilgrims from the west, who endowed them with lands in Europe from which they would get an income to help pay their clergy, repair their buildings, and assist their poor. Donors included some of the Byzantine emperors and the emperor Charlemagne. Once a year, on Palm Sunday, there was a great procession through the city from church to church, led by the patriarch. For the rest of the year, festival days in the Christian calendar were allowed to be celebrated at only one church for each festival.

After the earthquake of 1033, the city walls had to be rebuilt. Although Ramleh was the administrative capital of the Muslim province of Palestine, the official administration moved to Jerusalem, which had come through the earthquake in better shape. The Christians were told by the governor that they would have to pay their share of the costs. They wrote to the Byzantine emperor for help, pleading that they were too poor. The emperor offered to pay the caliph for the Christians' share of the new wall on condition that it protect only that part of the city in which Christians lived. So when the new fortifications were finished in 1063, Jerusalem had its own Christian quarter.

The Christian population of Jerusalem may not have liked having to defer to their Muslim conquerors, but Muslim rule was thought by many to be the lesser of two evils. In the tenth century, when the people learned that the Greek Orthodox leader, the patriarch Johannes, had asked the Byzantine emperor to reconquer Jerusalem, the idea was so unpopular that he was killed in a riot. Even as second-class citizens, the ordinary Christian people seem to have preferred their Muslim rulers to the Byzantine rulers. The Muslim government was seen as less corrupt, and it levied lower taxes.

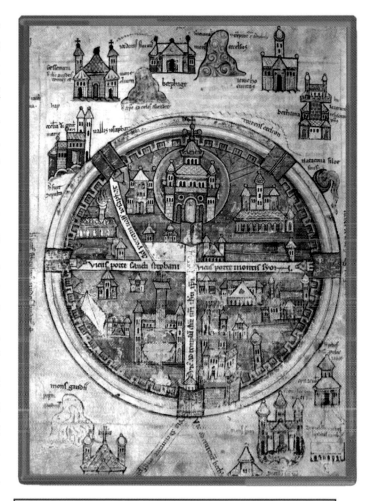

A map of Jerusalem from the *Chronicles of the Crusades* by Robert le Moine de Reims, a French abbot who was present at the conquest of the city in AD 1099

The Invaders

As news reached Jerusalem of the approach of the crusader army in 1096, it must have seemed that at last the prophecies about the end of the world were coming true. Some Jewish rabbis had calculated that the Messiah would come one thousand years after the destruction of the temple in Jerusalem by the Romans in the year AD 70. Others calculated the date of the Messiah's

A Jewish family holding a Passover celebration, from a fourteenth-century Spanish manuscript. There was a large population of Jews in Jerusalem before the crusaders arrived.

coming as 1085 or 1104. Some Muslim scholars thought that the end of the world would come in 1107, five hundred years after the death of Muhammad.

Refugees fled south in increasing numbers, with horrifying tales of the killing, looting, and burning done by the crusaders in the north. In 1096, Menachem ben Elijah wrote from somewhere near Constantinople: "I saw the troops of the Ashkenazim [the westerners] moving in their masses, and I do not know where they will turn next . . . " He added that he had intended to travel to Palestine but had decided it was too dangerous.

There had been earthquakes in the area in 1016, 1034, and 1067, the last one killing twenty-five thousand people in nearby Ramleh alone. Then, as cities like Jaffa fell to the crusaders, many Jews and Christians alike must have found refuge within Jerusalem's strong fortifications. Perhaps they thought that the city's holiness would protect them. The city's population may have doubled, perhaps to as much as one hundred and fifty thousand.

Soon war became not just a rumor but a fact. In the summer of 1098, the Egyptians took Jerusalem from the Seljuk Turks after a siege lasting forty days. The new military governor of the city, Iftikhar Al-Daulah, had forty siege engines, catapults on wheeled platforms that could hurl heavy rocks. He had used these to take the city, and he could now use them as artillery to protect the city. He had only a few hundred professional soldiers to defend the city, so he instructed them to supervise all the citizens in strengthening the city's defenses. Everyone had to help the soldiers and patrol those sections of the walls nearest their homes.

The looting of Jerusalem after its capture by Christian crusaders in 1099, from a fifteenth-century French illuminated manuscript

On June 7, 1099, sentries on Jerusalem's battlements could see the advance guard of the crusader army, which had reached a nearby hill to the north. The city soon fell, and the victorious crusaders slaughtered the population, Christians and Jews as well as Muslims. For so many, the end of the world had arrived.

Glossary

Bedouin   Desert nomads, organized in tribes. Bedouins often raided travelers and levied heavy tolls on merchants and pilgrims.

Byzantine   From Byzantium (Constantinople, modern Istanbul), capital of the Christian Greek emperors.

caliph   A Muslim ruler claiming religious and political authority because of his descent from Muhammad.

colonnade   A covered walkway or veranda, often surrounding a courtyard. A colonnade is open to the air, and the roof is held up by columns.

Damascene   From Damascus, the capital of Syria, famous for its fine metalwork.

dhimm   A Jew or a Christian protected by Islamic law (plural dhimmi).

Fatimid   An Arab dynasty of caliphs ruling Egypt and the neighboring countries at this time, named after Muhammad's daughter Fatima, the mother of the founder of the dynasty.

jizya   The tax paid by non-Muslims to their Muslim rulers.

Karaite   A Jewish sect that rejected the authority of rabbis.

kharaj The Muslim land tax.

musk An expensive perfume derived from the scent glands of a kind of deer.

Orthodox The conservative, traditional form of a religion, often also referring to the beliefs of the majority.

patriarch A senior Greek Orthodox bishop.

Rabbainite A Jewish sect that followed the traditional teachings of the rabbis.

Seljuk A Turkish dynasty of caliphs ruling Iraq and neighboring countries.

Shia A sect of Islam, differing from the Sunni over the true line of descent of the caliphs.

sultan Muslim term for an emperor. In theory, it is the ruler of all Muslims; a Seljuk ruling from Baghdad in Iraq.

Sunni Orthodox Muslims.

Torah The Jewish holy book; the first five books of the Bible.

turban Cloth headgear that is wound around the head; its size denoted the social rank of the wearer.

For More Information

The Columbia University Medieval Guild
602 Philosophy Hall, Columbia University
New York, NY 10027
e-mail: cal36@columbia.edu
Web site: http://www.cc.columbia.edu/cu/medieval

The Dante Society of America
Brandeis University
P.O. Box 549110
Waltham, MA 02454-9110
e-mail: dsa@dantesociety.org
Web site: http://www.dantesociety.org

International Courtly Literature Society
North American Branch
c/o Sara Sturm-Maddox
Department of French and Italian
University of Massachusetts at Amherst
Amherst, MA 01003
e-mail: ssmaddox@frital.umass.edu
Web site: http://www-dept.usm.edu/~engdept/icls/
    iclsnab.htm

Medieval Academy of America
1430 Massachusetts Avenue
Cambridge, MA 02138
(617) 491-1622
e-mail: speculum@medievalacademy.org
Web site: http://www.medievalacademy.org

Rocky Mountain Medieval and Renaissance Association
Department of English Language and Literature
University of Northern Iowa
Cedar Falls, IA 50614-0502
(319) 273-2089
e-mail: jesse.swan@uni.edu
Web site: http://www.uni.edu/~swan/rmmra/rocky.htm

Web Sites

Due to the changing nature of Internet links, the Rosen Publishing Group, Inc., has developed an online list of Web sites related to the subject of this book. This site is updated regularly. Please use this link to access the list:

http://www.rosenlinks.com/lma/jumr

For Further Reading

Goitein, S. D. *Letters of Medieval Jewish Traders*. Princeton, NJ: Princeton University Press, 1973.

Hallam, Elizabeth, ed. *Chronicles of the Crusades: Eye-Witness Accounts of the Wars between Christianity and Islam*. Godalming, UK: Bramley Books, 1997.

Le Strange, Guy, trans. *I-Khusrau, Nasir: Diary of a Journey through Syria and Palestine in 1047 AD*. New York: Palestine Pilgrims' Text Society, 1971.

Le Strange, Guy, ed. and trans. *Mukaddassi: Description of Syrian and Palestine*. New York: Palestine Pilgrims' Text Society, 1971.

Le Strange, Guy. *Palestine Under the Muslims: A Description of Syria and the Holy Land from AD 650 to 1500*. Beirut: Khayats, 1965.

Prawer, Joshua, and Haggai Ben-Shammai. *The History of Jerusalem: The Early Muslim Period 639–1099*. New York: New York University Press, 1996.

Bibliography

Armstrong, Karen. *A History of Jerusalem: One City, Three Faiths*. London: Harper Collins, 1996.

Belaev, E. A. *Arabs, Islam and the Arab Caliphate in the Early Middle Ages*. New York: Praeger Inc., 1995.

Courbage, Youssef, and Philippe Faigues. *Christians and Jews Under Islam*. New York: I. B. Tams, 1997.

Frank, Daniel, ed. *The Jews of Medieval Islam: Community, Society and Identity*. New York: E. J. Brill, 1995.

Goitein, S. D. *Letters of Medieval Jewish Traders*. Princeton, NJ: Princeton University Press, 1973.

Hallam, Elizabeth, ed. *Chronicles of the Crusades: Eye-Witness Accounts of the Wars between Christianity and Islam*. Godalming, UK: Bramley Books, 1997.

Holtz, Avraham, ed. *The Holy City: Jews on Jerusalem*. New York: Norton, 1971.

Idinopulos, Thomas A. *Jerusalem: A History of the Holiest City as Seen Through the Struggles of Jews, Christians and Muslims*. Chicago: Ivan R. Dee, 1994.

Le Strange, Guy, trans. *I-Khusrau, Nasir: Diary of a Journey through Syria and Palestine in 1047 AD.* New York: Palestine Pilgrims' Text Society, 1971.

Le Strange, Guy. *Palestine Under the Muslims: A Description of Syria and the Holy Land from AD 650 to 1500.* Beirut, Khayats, 1965.

Prawer, Joshua. *The History of the Jews in the Latin Kingdom of Jerusalem.* Oxford, UK: Clarendon Press, 1988.

Prawer, Joshua, and Haggai Ben-Shammai. *The History of Jerusalem: The Early Muslim Period 639–1099.* New York: New York University Press, 1996.

Tritton, A. S. *The Caliphs and Their Muslim Subjects.* London: Frank Cass & Co., 1970.

Index

About the Author

Nick Ford studied comparative religion at the University of Lancaster and recently gained a first class Joint Honors degree from the Open University in European humanities and classical studies. He is currently engaged in part-time postgraduate research at the University of Southampton. He has also worked for fifteen years as a costumed interpreter at a number of historical sites in Britain, has written papers on medieval and Roman history, and particularly enjoys studying the religion and everyday life of both periods. He lives in Southampton with his wife, Carol, and two cats, Ted and Rosie.

Photo Credits

Cover © Sonia Halliday Photographs; p. 4 © Jane Taylor/Sonia Halliday Photographs; p. 8 © AKG London; p. 9 © Prue Grice/ Sonia Halliday Photographs; pp. 10, 22 © Christie's Image LTD; p. 12 © François Guènet/ AKG London; p. 16 © Real Biblioteca de lo Escorial/Dagli Orti/The Art Archive; pp. 17, 19, 21 © LotFinder; pp. 28, 31, 32, 40, 44 © British Library/The Art Archive; p. 36 © Bibliothèque Nationale Paris/Dagli Orti/The Art Archive; p. 39 © Biblioteca Nacional Lisbon/Dagli Orti/The Art Archive; p. 41 © Palatine Library Parma/Dagli Orti/The Art Archive; p. 42 © Bodleian Library Oxford/The Bodleian Library/The Art Archive; pp. 46, 49 © Erich Lessing/AKG London; p. 51 © Uppsala University Library Sweden/Dagli Orti/The Art Archive; p. 52 © British Library/AKG London; p. 54 © The Bridgeman Art Library.

Designer: Geri Fletcher; **Editor:** Jake Goldberg; **Photo Researcher:** Elizabeth Loving